3 EASY HABITS for Network Marketing

AUTOMATE YOUR MLM SUCCESS

KEITH & TOM "BIG AL" SCHREITER

3 Easy Habits for Network Marketing
© 2016 by Keith & Tom "Big Al" Schreiter

Published by Fortune Network Publishing
PO Box 890084
Houston, TX 77289 USA
Telephone: +1 (281) 280-9800

ISBN-10:1-892366-69-X
ISBN-13:978-1-892366-69-6

CONTENTS

PREFACE.

Want to know a secret?

Want to grow your business without stress and massive willpower?

Want to build your business 24 hours a day, even while you sleep?

Here's the secret:

Habits.

We might think habits are boring, but here is what happened to me.

I was having lunch with Steve Scott, an expert on habits. Steve explained how habits transformed his life.

And then, I got it.

Habits are automatic! They are painless! We don't even notice that we are doing them.

Habits are easy because ... well, they are already a habit.

So here is our plan:

1. Create a new habit (this is one-time work).
2. Put our new habit on autopilot.
3. Allow our new habit to build our business automatically.

Pretty simple concept.

Thank you, Steve, for making this so clear.

—Tom "Big Al" Schreiter

HOW THIS BOOK WORKS.

First, we will learn a little bit about how habits work. (Just an overview. There are already many great books on the science of habits.)

Second, we will learn how to create habits that will make our network marketing success more automatic.

Third, we will discover little tricks and shortcuts that will increase our chances of successfully building habits.

Is learning a new habit worth it?

We like this excerpt from a newsletter by Nick Stephenson when he talks about his son:

"My eldest son learned to walk over 18 months ago. And he has continued the habit.

"But what we often forget is, he spent over 12 months failing miserably at it. Then, one day, he had failed enough times that he knew how to do it properly."

So let's get ready to learn more about how habits work.

THE SECRET POWER OF HABITS.

We developed the habit of putting on clothes before leaving our house.

How many times have we missed it? None that we can remember.

Our habits get done automatically.

No willpower needed.

And that is the secret of this book.

Good habits.

- Following up with our best prospects.
- Returning telephone calls promptly.
- Seeing prospects in person.
- Making time for personal development every day.
- Being open-minded.
- Listening attentively.
- Making a to-do list.
- Being on time, every time.
- Telling stories, not just facts.
- Promoting events.

Bad habits.

- Doing just the minimum.
- Surrounding ourselves with negative people.
- Forgetting our top priorities.
- Putting off our most important tasks.
- Criticizing others.
- Mindlessly watching TV as the hours go by.
- Not attending company events.
- Avoiding exercise.
- Not setting goals.

Gee, that was easy.

Habits are easy to list and talk about. Talk is cheap.

This is not our challenge!

Our challenge is to **create** new habits that serve us. We want habits that automatically move us toward our goals. Yes, our habits can make us successful.

THE GOOD NEWS
AND THE BAD NEWS.

First, the good news.

The good news is that habits can change our lives. Habits can put our success on autopilot. And habits can make distasteful activities happen without using massive amounts of willpower.

In other words, habits are awesome.

Now, for the bad news.

The bad news is that habits don't just happen by themselves. They will take effort. If you are reading this book, you probably have a full-time career, a family, a social life, and a network marketing business.

Setting goals, being positive, creating new habits and learning new people skills can all be overwhelming.

Think big. Start small.

Relax. In this book, we are only going to ask you to create one new habit at a time. That's it.

Why? Because if we understand how habits are formed, we can create new steps and a new habit. Then, we will have our own personal template to create all the additional habits we want.

Just create one new habit. Watch how that habit builds our network marketing business automatically, with almost no effort on our part. When we see this happening, we will be addicted to creating new habits.

For example, let's say that we are afraid of making telephone calls to prospects. What if these calls became natural and automatic? What if these calls were easy and just part of our daily routine? Maybe they will become as natural as brushing our teeth in the morning.

Now, that would be exciting. No more stress. No more strenuous willpower. Those telephone calls are now just part of our normal daily routine.

We want to replace difficult activities with naturally-occurring habits.

WILLPOWER IS HIGHLY OVERRATED.

Habits are more important than goals.

Goals take willpower every day. If we depend on willpower, we are finished.

Our conscious mind only has a limited amount of willpower each day. We use that willpower up quickly. And then, during the rest of the day, we fall back into our regular habits. Just think how easy it is to fall into our old bad habits in the evening when we are tired.

Habits happen naturally. It is just what we do. It is our "default setting."

Need some examples of running out of willpower? When we run out of willpower during the day, we automatically default to:

- Mindlessly watching television until we are too tired to watch anymore.
- Eating snacks and junk food because they are convenient and we are too tired to make or get better food.
- Listening to music to unwind.
- Surfing the Internet to pass the time.
- Rescheduling the "To-Do" list for the 100th time.

- Lazily setting new goals that we will never act on.
- Daydreaming about what could happen if our dreams ever came true.

And now, time just slips by. The day is gone. Our automatic habits just ran on autopilot and finished out our day.

Willpower is limited.

Willpower comes from the conscious mind, the weakest part of our brain. This takes energy. And if the task or goal is huge, this will take more mind energy than we have each day.

Thinking our way to success is a bad plan.

Habits are automatic.

As we've seen, when we are tired, we default to our automatic habits. Even if we are tired, we do our programmed habits such as:

- Brushing our teeth.
- Taking a shower.
- Eating.
- Tying our shoes before walking.
- Driving on the correct side of the road.
- Starting the day with a cup of coffee.
- Ending the day with a bowl of ice cream.
- Smiling when we say "Hi" to a stranger.

- Holding the telephone with our dominant hand.
- Showing up for work five minutes late.
- Leaving work five minutes early.
- Taking the same route home from work.
- Shopping at the same store for supplies.
- Checking our social media when we get to work.
- Taking the same amount of donuts during our break.
- Putting our left shoe on first in the morning.
- Throwing our dirty clothes in the same spot at night.
- Reacting to impolite drivers in the same way.
- Watching the same weekly series on television.
- Checking the same websites daily.
- Taking our work breaks at the same time.
- Avoiding tidying up our desk.
- Reading the morning paper.

Yes, we live a programmed routine. Most of the things we do are simply habits.

WHO ARE WE?

We are a collection of our habits.

Sure, we can consciously change our attitude or activity through sheer willpower. But, willpower weakens. Eventually our default habits take over.

Look at Mary. Is she consistently happy? She created the habit of reacting to the events in her life with a happy perspective.

What about Bill? Is he consistently complaining? Then he created the habit of focusing on the negative aspects of the events in his life.

No matter how hard we try with willpower, our habits will take over the moment our willpower is weak. Willpower is difficult to maintain, and we tire quickly.

That is why habits are important in network marketing. The habits we build can consistently move us forward to our goals.

We are on autopilot.

Our conscious minds can manage one thought at a time. That's it. Whatever we focus on, we can control that thought.

Unfortunately, we must make hundreds of decisions every minute, just to keep us alive. And all these decisions are made automatically by the subconscious mind.

What is the subconscious mind?

Here is a simple explanation that we can use for our study of habits. Our subconscious mind is "a collection of automatic programs and habits."

So almost everything we do is a program or habit we have developed over time. Some examples of these automatic decisions?

- Open the left chamber of the heart for blood to move.
- Move 40% of nerve energy to this muscle.
- Blink this eye.
- Create 30,000 new digestive enzymes.
- Tighten the thigh muscle to keep our balance.
- Initiate another breath.
- Smile at the person passing by.
- Say, "Oh no, I'm just looking," to the sales clerk.
- Keep the car in the correct lane while concentrating on the music from the radio.
- Turn at the intersection where we always turn.
- Curse at the alarm clock.
- Be skeptical with salespeople.
- Sprinkle salt on our food using our right hand.
- Remove weak T4 cells.

- Put on our underwear before our clothes.
- Sit in the same place for lunch.
- Have the same whining conversation at the coffee machine.
- Check how we look when passing a mirror.

The list can go on and on. All of these decisions were automatic, outside of our conscious control and willpower.

We truly are a collection of our habits. We live our lives on autopilot.

Change our habits, change our lives.

If we want to change our lives, we simply change our programs and habits. Then, the changes will happen automatically, without the need for strenuous willpower.

We can rest, just like the commercial jet pilots do, when their autopilot settings fly the plane flawlessly for hours.

And like the airline pilot, we can choose how to program our autopilot settings to get where we want. Our job is to develop new habits, and let our new habits take us where we want to go.

Can autopilot work in our network marketing business?

Absolutely! In fact, this is the best and most efficient way to build our business. We have habits because they are natural and easy to do. It is our default setting.

Do you want to enjoy the process of building your network marketing career? Of course. So why not make the process enjoyable and natural? And automatic!

No need to feel guilty when our willpower gives out. Instead, we will depend on our habits to comfortably take us to our goals.

Will it be difficult or uncomfortable to create new habits?

The simple techniques in this book will make it easier. New habits will require effort and skill, but think of the alternative. If we rely on making conscious willpower decisions forever ... well, that is just too hard. New habits are the best way to get us to our goals.

Need a few simple examples of creating a new habit?

Shaving. If we normally start shaving the left side of our face, we have created a habit. It will feel weird to start shaving the right side of our face first.

But, start shaving the right side of our face first, and in just one week, this will feel normal and comfortable. New habit. Simple.

Or, clasp our hands together and see which thumb is on top. Is it our right? Is it our left? Unclasp and now switch them, placing the opposite thumb on top. Most people will say this feels a bit odd.

Wait another 30 seconds, do it again. Now it feels a little less weird. Unclasp and do it again and again. Soon, the weird feeling doesn't come back. Now it feels more normal. Maybe it is not a habit yet, but we are making progress.

Yes, we can create new habits. Some habits develop quickly. Other habits take time. For example, a young lady starts carrying a purse. In the beginning, she forgets and often leaves her purse behind. After a few months, remembering to take the purse becomes automatic.

I remember my first cellphone. It was easy to leave behind in restaurants and friends' homes. It took months to develop the habit of remembering to pick up my cellphone before leaving.

Does it take 21 days to create a habit?

Obviously not. It took months to consistently remember the purse or cellphone. Yet, put a hand on a hot stove burner, and we create an instant habit to never put a hand on a stove burner again.

It is not the length of time that creates a habit. The two major factors that build habits are:

1. How important the result is to you.

2. The intensity of the experience.

So doing something over and over again helps, but it won't guarantee a lifelong habit.

But there is some good news about creating one new habit.

The domino effect.

As children, we played with dominoes. A fun activity was to set up 10, 100 or even 1,000 dominoes close together. Then, push the first domino and watch each domino topple the next domino in our creation.

The world record stands at 500,000 dominoes toppling over sequentially. Quite a record. But the best part is that we only have to push over the first domino. The chain reaction happens with no further effort or input from us.

This domino effect was noted in a Northwestern University Medical study. This study showed that changing one bad habit had a domino effect on other bad habits.

The domino effect in real life.

Mike decides to lose weight. He won't chance failure by attempting to use willpower to achieve his weight loss. No, he will change just one habit, and then let the domino effect automatically cascade to create new habits in his life. Here is his plan:

1. He'll start small. He won't pick something hard. Just a tiny new habit that will have the best chance of success.

2. Instead of starving himself, withholding food, or pumping iron at the local gym, Mike decides on an easy first step. He decides to create a new habit of waking up 20 minutes earlier each day.

3. To compensate for any difficulty, Mike can adjust by going to bed 20 minutes earlier at night.

4. When Mike wakes up early, all he has to do is to take a short 20-minute walk.

5. Mike enjoys his quiet time during his 20-minute walk every morning. During his leisurely walk he plans his day, clears his mind, or if he prefers, just listens to his favorite music.

One year later, Mike is 40 pounds lighter.

The domino effect for Mike.

Did that short 20-minute walk burn that many calories? No.

Was the 20-minute walk the biggest factor in weight loss? No.

So what happened?

The new 20-minute walk habit set off a chain reaction. During his walk, Mike thought about his choices. He gradually started watching what he ate. He began to eat a little less at night. He drank less beer when he returned from work.

Was this hard at first? A bit, but not overwhelming. After all, it was just a 20-minute walk the first thing in the morning.

Mike noticed that he felt better during the day. He had more energy all day long. And, Mike felt bad on the days he missed his treasured morning walk.

Over time, Mike experienced less stress, took fewer medications, spent less money on beer, and spent less money on sodas and other stimulants. These new habits came from a simple decision to wake up 20 minutes earlier for a leisurely walk. This one simple decision set off a chain reaction which led Mike to success.

But what about our network marketing business?

Could we begin with a daily 15-minute activity that could start this domino effect in our network marketing business? Or how about starting with just a five-minute activity? Or if that is too hard, a two-minute activity?

We are the pilot. We can set our autopilot to do the automatic activity for us when we create the proper habit.

Just like the pilot, it all starts with us. Magic won't happen unless we do something to start. We have to decide:

1. Where we are going.

2. The daily activities or habits we want.

3. And if needed, we will need to learn the necessary skills to make our daily habits effective.

Habits are awesome.

Habits are our friends.

Habits will propel us towards our goals … automatically.

HABIT #1: PERSONAL DEVELOPMENT.

Let's start by creating an easy habit. Will this be the only habit we develop? Of course not.

But the tips and strategies in this book will make more sense once we look at this first example of creating a habit.

"I want to be more positive."

This might be our first challenge when we start our network marketing career. Yes, we get a bit accustomed to our negative environment.

Negative news on television, negative comments on the Internet, negative conversations at work, negative social circles ... it all adds up. This accumulation of negativity limits our belief in our potential.

The antidote? Personal development.

Negative impressions limit our ability to believe in the new possibilities afforded by network marketing.

We need to balance this overload of negative impressions. How?

By exposing ourselves to positive personal development.

Top leaders in network marketing seem so positive. Of course it is easy for them to believe in possibilities; they've already experienced the possibilities.

However, the top leaders didn't start off with total belief in themselves and their businesses. They developed this attitude over time. How?

- They listened to motivational audios.
- They read biographies of successful people.
- They attended workshops and seminars.
- They associated with more positive people when possible.

These leaders did these activities consistently. They turned these activities into habits.

"I don't have time to do that."

Ah, but this is where habits come to the rescue! Excuses work when we deal with the conscious mind, when we have to think over a decision.

But habits? They just happen automatically.

What is the easiest excuse we can use to keep from investing time into personal development?

"I don't have time to do that."

Guess what? None of us have time. We are all busy with our lives, families, work and our everyday activities.

So instead of fighting this excuse with willpower, we will install a new habit into our lives.

Still not convinced that you have time to form a new habit? Well, how much time do you waste every day talking about the weather?

Or how much time do you waste on social media, looking at pictures of what your distant friends ate for lunch?

Habits happen.

Instead of trying to "make time," we could add a habit to our daily routine.

I have a friend named Alejandro. Every morning when he takes a shower, he listens to self-development audios. Instead of listening to music or just silence, he fills his mind with new beliefs and skills to move him forward in his career.

How much effort and willpower does this take? None. It is easy.

He has to shower and prepare for the day anyway. All he needs to do is hit "Play" on his phone and listen while he prepares. A more positive outlook and new ideas are sent to his brain effortlessly.

Another friend, David, has a passion for understanding how the human mind makes decisions. He finds it more enjoyable to read a book on this subject than watch late-night television. Every evening he improves his knowledge and understanding of the human mind. He doesn't miss the negative input of the late-night news.

How much effort and willpower does this take? None. It is easy. David enjoys reading.

My father hates to exercise. He will never run, because he finds it boring and thinks it requires too much effort. It would be impossible for him to create that habit.

However, he does enjoy listening to audios about marketing. Now he can take a walk while listening to his marketing audios, and improve his health while improving his mind. Walking is easy. And it is not boring when listening to a subject he finds interesting.

How much effort and willpower does this take? None. It is easy. He has to listen to something while he walks.

Do we know anyone who commutes to work? Instead of listening to and memorizing depressing lyrics to country-western songs, they could listen to inspiring stories on audio.

Most people have a lunch break at work. Instead of eating with negative co-workers who complain about their lives, they could go on a walk instead and listen to positive ideas on audio.

We might be thinking, "Hey, I could even keep a book with positive quotes in the bathroom!"

None of the above habits will take any extra time out of our day. And all of these activities can become natural, fun habits.

Today, most books and audios can be delivered directly to a portable device. We don't have to carry a physical book with us. We can't even use the "inconvenience" excuse any more.

Make this sample example work.

Remember our goal for this sample example? We wanted to become more positive.

So let's install a new habit to make that happen. From just the above examples, we have lots of options. But here is the option we choose:

Listen to self-development audios while preparing for the day.

Why did we choose this option?

#1. Easy. We can listen with no effort.

#2. Doesn't take any extra time out of our day. No willpower needed.

#3. Happens first thing in the morning. There is a better chance this habit will actually develop if we put it into action earlier in the day. If we wait until later in the day, there are too many other activities that could derail our new habit.

#4. This is easy to insert into our daily routine.

No stress, no rejection. This new habit is going to be easy. After one or two weeks of pressing "Play" as soon as we start our morning preparation, this habit will seem as natural as brushing our teeth.

Bottom line?

We improve our positive outlook. Done.

MAKING THIS HABIT HAPPEN!

We are anxious to start this new habit of morning personal development. But this habit won't just magically happen because we're thinking about it. We have to plan. We have to make the performance of this habit inevitable.

Here are a few things that we can do to increase the chances that we install this habit into our lives.

#1. If we are going to listen to personal development audios on our cellphone, let's buy some inexpensive speakers. Now we can listen to our audios while we are in the noisy shower.

#2. Order a variety of different personal development audios. Maybe an audio on goals, and another audio on motivation. With a variety of topics, we will never be bored.

#3. Include audios on skill development. Programming our mind for success is great, but we also want to learn the skills to execute our new programs. Include audios that teach us how to talk to prospects, how to close, how to create interest, how to lead, etc.

#4. Always charge the device that plays our audios in the area where we prepare ourselves each morning. That way our device is already in position for us to start playing our audios. Maybe we will place it by our toothbrush, or better yet, by our alarm clock.

#5. Reward ourselves with our favorite cup of coffee or breakfast drink. Make sure we have some personal development reading material while we enjoy our morning coffee in the kitchen. That could mean discontinuing our negative newspaper subscription. Instead, we have a book from our favorite motivational author.

#6. As our habit becomes stronger, we may want to extend our personal development time. Now we invest in a good set of headphones so that we can listen to our audios while commuting on the train to work. If we drive, we will make sure we have plenty of audios in our car.

#7. Do we like to challenge our brains? Then make sure that some of our audios will teach us new information. We could learn things such as how our brains work. Or, new ways of engaging with prospects. We want to make our personal development interesting so that we will continue this habit.

#8. Use an affirmation. This is another way to assist in the development of our new habit. We affirm to ourselves that we are a person that possesses that habit. What we are saying to ourselves is, "I am the type of person that does these things." In this case, we would affirm to ourselves throughout the day, "I am a personal development enthusiast. I love personal development."

Want to make these affirmations stronger? Just remind ourselves often with notes on our mirror, our television, our refrigerator, our computer, etc.

#9. Associate with people who share our passion for personal development. Jim Rohn was famous for saying, "You are the average of the five people you spend the most time with." If we associate with people who think like we do, we will enjoy our conversations. Gradually we will spend less time with people who gossip, talk about negative situations, and complain about the pain of being victims.

Starting to see a trend?

We are putting our efforts into focusing on just one habit. We want to make this habit permanent. This will take time.

It is easy to lose our focus, and we may want to accomplish many habits simultaneously. This is usually counterproductive. Habits take focus and repetition.

Let's look a bit at the power of focus.

HOW DO WE DEVELOP HABITS?

"Old habits die hard!"

"You can't teach an old dog new tricks!"

Are these accurate phrases? Most of the time, yes.

It is easier to quote a phrase than to take personal responsibility. But we want to change, right?

Then, how do we get our old habits to die so that we can learn new habits or tricks?

First, forget about the past. Stop thinking about our current bad habits.

Second, totally focus on a new habit. When our mind is 100% focused on the new replacement habit, there is no room for our old habit to exist.

The case study to help us forget the past, and focus on the future.

In the 2012 Summer Olympics road race, Rigoberto Uran was about to win the gold medal. He was only a few hundred meters from the finish line. He only had one other competitor challenging him for the win.

But, with only 300 meters to go, Rigoberto made a huge mistake. He glanced over his left shoulder to check the progress of his competitor. This brief and temporary break in his stride allowed his competitor, Alexander Vinokourov, to pass him and ... Alexander won the gold medal.

What happened?

Alexander Vinokourov focused entirely on the future, the finish line. He won the gold medal.

Rigoberto Uran focused on the past, and unfortunately, left the Olympics with the silver medal. Instead of focusing on the finish line, he decided to look behind him.

Focus: Priority #1.

Creating a new habit won't happen if it is only a fleeting thought. New habits take time and commitment. We need to keep our attention on our new habit until it is automatic.

CAN I SUCCEED IN CREATING NEW HABITS?

Here is the good news. We already know how to create new habits. We've created new habits all our lives.

Our current habits are what brought us to where we are today.

We created habits of showering, brushing our teeth, tying our shoes, and more.

How did we do this?

Focus. And focusing was easy because we deeply desired to create a new skill or habit.

We learned to walk.

Infants decide they want to walk. They make a decision when the time is right for them.

Why do they decide to walk? Many reasons.

- They want to be like everyone else.
- They think it may be fun.
- It is a faster way to get from one place to another.
- It is a new challenge.
- They believe it is possible. They see others walking.

Do they succeed the first time they try walking? No. They meet a 100% failure rate the first time they try.

But, they have desire. Who knows how long they mentally prepare themselves to start walking?

Now comes the trial and error phase, failing and falling. It is a long process. But their desire pushes them forward.

Fast-forward a few months and they have developed what will be a lifelong habit of walking, and it is all automatic. They don't have to think about the process of walking again.

If we have trouble creating a new habit, maybe it is because we don't want it badly enough yet.

So, let's make sure we want the habit of personal development.

WHY FOCUS ON PERSONAL DEVELOPMENT FIRST?

#1. We can create our personal development habit immediately. We don't have to drive to a gym, put on workout clothes, or make an appointment to get started right away.

#2. We don't have to wait for our accountability partner to be available. This is a habit that we can do ourselves.

#3. Physical exercise can give us sore muscles the next day. That would give us a built-in excuse not to exercise the second day. But there is no trauma involved in listening to personal development audios. Ear injuries are rare.

#4. We all have "wasted time" during the day. Sometimes it is only a few minutes, sometimes longer. Listening to a personal development audio is easy to do during these periods of "wasted time." For example, we could listen to some personal development audios while standing in line at lunch. Now, we couldn't put on our jogging clothes to exercise during this time. But, we can listen to an audio on goals rather than staring off into space.

#5. Personal development helps us build a stronger self-image. Our self-image is how we see ourselves. Here is a good example:

Imagine a person who has been unemployed for years. This person spends the day watching soap operas on television while eating chips. One day this person receives a million-dollar gift from an unknown donor. Where is that person three years later? Broke. Watching television and eating chips. Why? Because this person did not grow personally into a millionaire.

To become a millionaire, we have to grow into the type of person who would be a millionaire. Just giving someone a million dollars does not change the person.

Or, let's look at it another way. If someone is a self-made millionaire, and loses it all in a lawsuit, where is that person three years later? Back on top. Why? Because that person saw himself as a millionaire. The loss of his fortune was only a temporary event in his mind.

"If we want more, we have to become more."

There is a saying, "Money will only make us a bigger person of who we are." So if we are a jerk, money will just make us a bigger jerk. We have to change ourselves from the inside.

#6. Are we attractive?

Think about going to a party. Who do you want to have a conversation with? Someone who is positive, or someone who is negative?

Now think about potential prospects. Who do we think prospects want to associate with?

Someone who sees himself as a victim? Or, someone who looks for new possibilities and opportunities in life?

A constant deposit of personal development into our minds pays off big in our network marketing career. We will spend less time chasing prospects, and more time attracting prospects to us.

As a bonus, our personal lives will improve also. Our relationships will become more positive.

#7. Personal development is easy to scale up. In the beginning, we might only do five minutes a day. Later, we can extend our personal development time by reading a chapter of a good inspirational biography instead of watching the news.

Scale up?

Yes. By making our first habit stronger, other habits get easier. Remember the domino effect we talked about earlier?

WIN ON YOUR FIRST TRY.

Our chance of success is greater when we choose an easy habit. Less willpower. Fewer traumatic decisions. We can continue this new habit with minimal stress.

Install the easiest version of our new habit first. Then, we can scale up or "supersize" our new habit.

When we choose a personal development habit, we start with five or ten minutes a day while preparing for work. Once we establish this new habit, we can "supersize" our personal development time up to 15 minutes, 20 minutes, or even 30 minutes a day.

Just remember to make the increases in our "supersizing" small. Small adjustments won't require additional willpower.

Here is an easy way to remember to make our increases small. Imagine that we want to run a marathon. Now, 26 miles is a long way. If we try that on our first day, we will fail.

Instead, we will start small. If we are out of shape, then we will start with walking 10 minutes a day. Gradually we will increase our walking time. Eventually, we can start jogging. And finally, we can extend our jogging time a little bit every week until we are able to do a marathon.

Laura versus Mary.

Laura and Mary make a New Year's resolution to lose weight.

Laura goes all in. New clothes, new premium gym membership, new diet books, a complete overhaul of her pantry and refrigerator, a vision board and all the conscious willpower she can muster.

Day one. A diet of bread crumbs. A grueling two-hour workout.

Day two. Laura is starving. Every muscle in her body hurts. She can't reach her shoelaces. She cannot step into her car to go to work. So what does Laura do?

Laura skips her second day of workouts. Instead, she eats junk food and relaxes in front of her television.

Day three. Laura attempts a small workout, but quits because her body still hurts. Laura consoles herself with a donut.

Day four. Laura skips the workout and immediately reaches for the ice cream.

Day five. Laura quits her New Year's resolution. She tried, she failed, and her life is too busy for her commitment.

Laura gains weight.

Laura starts eating more donuts to combat her weight-gain stress.

What about Mary?

Mary starts small. Really small.

No gym membership. No new workout clothes. No restrictive diets. Just one small baby step for her first week to get in shape.

What does she do?

Week one. Instead of ordering French fries, she orders a roasted sweet potato for lunch. Every day that week, Mary substitutes a roasted sweet potato for French fries. Now, ordering a roasted sweet potato is a habit.

Week two. Mary loves watching television to unwind after work. Every night she enjoys two hours of her favorite shows. Now, Mary reduces her television-watching time by 30 minutes. So instead of 30 minutes of sitting, she invests that same 30 minutes into an activity that requires movement. This could be a walk, cleaning the house, or strolling the aisles of her favorite store.

Week three. Mary removes one donut from her morning coffee break. She substitutes a healthier snack. After just one week, her craving for that morning donut goes away. A new habit is born.

Mary begins to gradually lose weight. She feels better. Her new habits help her manage her weight automatically.

Small changes. Huge results.

HABIT #2.
MEET ONE NEW PERSON A DAY.

We can have a great attitude, a terrific self-image, and even great communication skills. However, if we have no one to talk to, we won't go far in our network marketing career.

Having more prospects is better than … having fewer prospects. Gee, that wasn't hard.

Having more prospects instantly increases our self-confidence. If our business success depends on just a few prospects, then we will display signs of anxiety and stress.

But what if we develop a huge reservoir of prospects? If we have one bad encounter with a prospect, then we won't feel bad. We will think, "Hey, I have ten more prospects to talk to this week and they will definitely be better than this negative prospect."

Our posture counts.

Think about how we appear to prospects. Do we appear desperate or confident?

What if we say to a prospect, "I tried calling. Didn't you get my 32 voicemail messages?" Well, this prospect smells desperation. No one wants to follow a desperate person.

However, what if we can calmly talk to a prospect and not feel desperate or needy? We think, "My time is limited. I can only sponsor and train a few people. I'd better choose motivated prospects."

Now we are more attractive to prospects. They don't sense desperation. They sense impending success.

It is easy to be confident when we have many prospects to choose from. But how do we build this massive list of prospects?

Just meet new people.

If we are introverts, meeting new people can be scary. That leaves us with two choices:

1. Continually go outside our comfort zone and feel uncomfortable every day that we work our business.

2. Learn new skills so that meeting one new person a day is within our comfort zone. Now we can enjoy doing our business every day.

Now, both options work. However, most people choose option number two: "Learning new skills."

If we dread the thought of meeting one new person a day, then how are we going to make this a habit?

Remember, we want our new habit to be automatic. We need to make meeting new people an enjoyable experience.

Start learning now.

Let's ask ourselves this question: "When is a good time to learn exactly what to say to a great prospect?"

- Before we meet the great prospect?
- Or after we meet the great prospect?

The answer is obvious.

And once we learn what to say, how do we become comfortable talking to prospects?

With practice. New distributors need experience talking to prospects.

Consider this example. A young man wants to ask a young lady for a date. If the young man has never asked for a date before, what would we expect to see?

- Nervousness.
- Stuttering.
- No confidence.
- Bad posture.
- Ugly results.

However, if the young man had months or years of experience asking for dates, wouldn't we expect his conversation to be better?

We would expect the young man to speak more confidently and to have better posture.

To make meeting one new person a day a comfortable habit, we have to do two things:

1. Learn what to say when meeting new people.

2. Practice saying these words to new prospects until we become comfortable.

How important is this habit to us?

If we want to be successful in our network marketing business, this habit is extremely important. We don't need more motivation. We just need to install this habit.

Why this habit will move our network marketing business forward.

Imagine we talk to 100 prospects. In that group of prospects, five prospects will never join. Their spirits were crushed by society. Their vampire bosses sucked out all of their dreams. They gave up hope and are just waiting to die.

In that same group of 100 prospects, we will also find five people who will join just because we showed up. They are at a point in their lives where they are looking for solutions. Our opportunity is the solution they are looking for. We wouldn't need much skill to get them on our team.

But what about those other 90 prospects? Well, we will need better communication skills to get our message inside their heads. We will learn these better communication skills as we progress in our network marketing business.

365 days a year = 365 new prospects for our business.

Meeting one new prospect a day is magic. If this seems scary, all we have to do is reframe this activity in our mind.

We like to say, "Go out and meet a new person. Don't try to sell him or her. Don't have an agenda. Instead, listen to how this person talks. Have fun analyzing which type of personality this person might be."

And why would we say that?

Because, as a new distributor, we may be worrying, "I hate talking to people with an agenda. I feel like I am making conditional friendships solely for the purpose of recruiting them into my business."

Instead, we can reframe this activity in our mind with this statement:

"I love talking to new people. They are interesting. A short conversation with new people is always fun. Maybe I can brighten their day. Maybe I will learn something new. Who can I say 'Hi' to next?"

Let's remove our agenda. Let's remove our business goals from our conversations. Instead, we just want to meet one new person a day to start getting the experience we need.

Now, if the conversation naturally leads to our product or business, let nature take its course. There is no rule that says we have to talk about business on our first conversation.

Do we feel better with this reframing?

Can we now have a more natural, stress-free conversation?

This should be rejection-free because there is nothing for our new friend to reject.

Meeting one new person a day is easy to talk about, but can we do this in real life? Let's see.

ONE PERSON A DAY!
ISN'T THAT A LOT TO ASK?

We don't have to stand in the middle of the street, accosting strangers. To have a short conversation with one new person a day is not difficult. Why not use a little imagination?

- Say "Hi" to the person behind you in line at the bank.
- Have a short message chat with a new friend on social media.
- Make a short telephone call to a referral.
- Attend a breakfast networking group.
- Accept an invitation to a party.
- Join an aerobics class and meet new people at the gym.
- Help a friend move to a new apartment and meet your friend's friends.
- Start taking walks on the local walking trail.
- Become a member of a local club.
- Go to a local attraction and take a tour. There are wine tours, historical tours, shopping tours and more.
- Check for local festivals in your area. Most cities will have an ethnic food festival, an art festival, and many special-interest festivals.

- Spend some time at the local flea market. Every weekend entrepreneur rents space to sell their items. You can talk to the vendors as well as the people attending.

- Do you have children? Make a point of attending their activities. You will meet other parents and have plenty of time to talk to them during the activities. Think dance classes, sports teams, concerts and more.

- How many local coffee shops are in your area? Not everyone comes into the coffee shop to sit down and stare at a cup of coffee. Many are looking forward to meeting new people. That could be you.

- Do you have a dog park in your area? Dog owners love talking to other dog owners. Dogs are great ice breakers. Don't have a dog? Offer to take your friend's or neighbor's dog.

- Do you garden? Ask for the advice of the clerk at the local gardening store.

- Like to read? Your local library has many activities for readers.

- Go to your local community college. They usually offer evening courses in computing, writing, marketing, business, and more. You can learn new things while meeting new classmates.

- Attend public seminars and educational events. Ask the person next to you, "What did you come here to learn?"

- Love music? Attend a local concert. Music lovers look forward to having conversations to share their passion about music.

- Shopping? Think of the possibilities of meeting sales clerks, other shoppers, and people conducting surveys in your local shopping mall.

- Join a local meetup group that focuses on travel. Travelers would love to have an extra passive income to extend their travel time. And if you sold nutritional products, join a group that caters to RV enthusiasts. This older crowd would have a keen interest in maintaining health.

- If you love golfing, go to the golf course alone. Let the local club pair you up with a new person, or better yet, put you into a foursome.

- If food and fine dining interest you, join a dinner club. You will have hours of relaxing time to visit with your fellow diners.

- Volunteer to help. Every organization needs new volunteers. Don't join with an agenda. Join to help. You will naturally meet new people.

Or ...

- Just hang around negative people. Instead of feeling sorry for them, why not create the habit of asking a question instead? When it is our turn to speak, we could comment on their problems by saying, "Would you like to do something about it?" Or, if that seems too forward, we could say, "Have you ever considered doing something about it?"

Of course most people would rather complain than look for a solution. However, some people might reply by asking us if we have a solution. Now people are asking us for solutions. Nice.

This isn't hard.

Anyone can improve their career by creating the habit of meeting new people. Some examples?

Eugene commutes daily on the train to his job. His bad habit? He gets depressed by reading the morning newspaper during his journey.

His new habit? Now he visits with his fellow commuters. He asks about their lives, their goals ... and even how they feel about waking up early to make the long commute to work.

Tammy usually surfs the Internet during her lunch break. The gossip sites are interesting. The pictures of cats are cute.

Now Tammy spends her lunch time making new friends on social media instead of reading stories about other people. Guess what? In a few months, Tammy will have over 300 new friends. That is plenty of new friends to move her business to the next level. This habit is so easy for Tammy. She still gets to spend lunch time on her computer.

Richard takes his daughter to her soccer practice and games. His conversations with the other parents usually went like this: "Nice weather we're having. Looks like a good day for practice." A nice, polite conversation.

Richard's new habit? When visiting during the games he says, "I market this new product that has this result. Do you know anyone that would like to have that result?"

By simply changing his conversation, Richard now has more prospects for his business. This did not take any more time. All it took was changing his old habit of idle chit-chat, and creating a new habit of asking this question.

Ann stopped ordering her products for home delivery. Instead, she now has her products delivered to her job. This is a great conversation-starter as her co-workers will ask, "And how is your business?" Easy.

Just small changes in our habits can compound our results over time.

THE SECRET?
NO AGENDA, NO PRESSURE.

We just need to put ourselves in position to meet new people. We can use our imagination to think of new and natural ways to contact new people.

Our fear of meeting new people evaporates when we don't have an agenda. Forcing a conversation to talk about our business can be uncomfortable, especially when we don't have the skills.

All we want this habit to do is make it easy for us to meet new people!

We are not asking too much of ourselves. We are not asking ourselves to do one presentation every day. We are not asking ourselves to meet lots of strangers daily.

We just want to meet one new person each day.

Some days will be easier than others. We might get lucky. Maybe on Monday we meet seven new people, and then we can take the rest of the week off.

BUT WHAT DO I SAY?

Step #1: Be in a position to meet new people.

Step #2: Say the right thing.

This formula is easy. We've already covered Step #1.

Now let's progress to the next step.

When we don't know what to say, fear will keep us from talking to new people. Like any new profession, network marketing requires that we learn new skills. Maybe we didn't learn good conversational skills in our previous career. If we haven't already, now would be a good time to make learning new conversation skills a priority in our lives.

There are many books and educational materials on how to be a better conversationalist. Let's look at a few good ways to start conversations now. We want to create the habit of talking to one new person a day.

Conversation starter #1.

This one is easy. All we have to do is … smile.

Our smile signals to a stranger that we are safe to approach. The stranger feels they could start a conversation with us with no rejection. With a simple smile, many strangers will start the conversation. We won't have to.

A smile is rejection-free. What is the worst that can happen? We smile at a person, and they don't smile back. Maybe their life is miserable. At least we contributed one smile to try and make their life better. We just move on.

However, this is what happens most of the time: We smile at someone we don't know, and the person smiles back. Both of us feel better.

Conversation starter #2.

"Hi" is a great start to any conversation. This doesn't sound abnormal or contrived. We say "Hi" every day, sometimes dozens of times a day. It is easy for a conversation to develop from there.

Conversation starter #3.

"How are you?" Or, "How are you doing?" Or, "How's it going?"

We have heard these phrases hundreds of times. These are non-threatening phrases, perfectly acceptable in conversation.

Conversation starter #4.

"I am just curious ..." This phrase is magic. What happens inside a stranger's head when he hears this phrase?

The stranger thinks, "What does this person want to know? I can help. What can I do to help this person?"

Some examples.

"I am just curious, have you been standing in this line long?"

"I am just curious, have you been a member of this organization for a long time?"

"I am just curious, is it easy to meet new people at this gym?"

Conversation starter #5.

Social media helps notify us of our friends' birthdays. Many of our so-called "friends" on social media are people we have never met. Here is an easy chance to connect with them. Instead of sending a simple text saying, "Happy Birthday!" ... we can do something different to stand out.

We can customize a photo. Or maybe we can find a resource that will connect with their interests and hobbies.

One of my friends, Jackie, sent me a birthday message that solicited a response. She said, "Happy birthday, Keith! How did you spend your special day?"

Not only was this message personalized, but adding a question at the end created a conversation.

Conversation starter #6.

"What did you do over the holidays?" This question is non-invasive. No one will feel threatened with this sort of conversation.

Now, we don't have to limit this question to just the holidays. We can talk about any event in the past. Here are some examples:

"What did you think was best about this lecture?"

"What did you learn from the seminar?"

"How long did it take you to get your license?"

"What did you like best about this event?"

Conversation starter #7.

At networking events, the common practice is to take someone's business card. Then, quickly move on to the next person. But the important thing is not the quantity of contacts that we make; it is the quality of the contacts we make.

Here are some questions that will engage our new contact. The more our new contact talks about himself, the stronger our connection. We won't be just one more business card discarded after the event.

"How did you get involved in your business?"

"Is this a pretty exciting business to be in?"

"How did you know about this networking event?"

"Tell me, what exactly does your business do?"

"What is the best part about being involved in your profession?"

"Do you go to other events like this?"

"What is the highlight of these events for you?"

"I don't know very many people here, so I wanted to introduce myself."

Conversation starter #8.

What are some safe questions that we can use to start conversations? What if we are around someone we don't know? We don't want to be intrusive. The following questions are socially acceptable and won't make it seem like we are deeply probing into someone's life.

"What do you do for a living?"

"How long have you been at your job?"

"What are you going to do when you retire?" (Might not be appropriate to someone younger.)

"Where do you live?"

"What is your dream job?"

"Where did you grow up?"

"Do you have any hobbies? What do you do in your free time?"

"How long does it take you to get to work?"

"What do you like to do on vacations or holidays?"

"What is your favorite restaurant here?"

"What is the best movie you have seen recently?"

"Do you have any trips coming up soon?"

"Do you have any pets?"

"Do you travel much?"

"So how is your day going?"

Conversation starter #9.

If we are shy, we are not alone. If we feel uncomfortable meeting new people, there will be many others who feel exactly like we do.

Imagine we are at a party, networking event, or other function. To stay within our comfort zone, all we have to do is to start conversations with shy people who are just like us.

Look around the room. Who are the people standing alone at the edges of the room? These people would love to have a conversation with someone, but they don't know how to start. Approach these people and say:

"Let me introduce myself. My name is _____. What's your name?"

"I am glad you are standing over here away from all the noise. My name is _____."

"Do you mind if I introduce myself? My name is _____."

"Do you mind if I join you over here? It is so loud by the bar."

"Do you know the organizer of this event?"

"Do you know when the food buffet opens? I don't know about you, but I am starving."

"Do you know what time this event ends?"

Don't be creepy.

When we meet new people, we want to make a good first impression. We don't want them to feel uncomfortable. Avoid questions such as:

"If you could be a fictional character, which one would you be?"

"If you were to die in the next 60 minutes, what would you regret the most?"

"Tell me the one secret you don't want anyone to know."

"What is the strangest thing you have ever done?"

"Have you ever stolen anything? Have you ever been caught?"

"What do you think is your purpose in life?"

"Met any aliens lately?"

"Do you hear little voices in your head also?"

"If you were stranded on a deserted island, who would be the one person you would want to be stranded with?"

These questions assume a lot more familiarity. We don't have that yet when we first meet someone. Stick with safe questions.

Make sure to share a little bit about ourselves between our questions. We don't want to make this sound like an interrogation.

Bottom line?

Meet one new person.

We become comfortable with repetition. By developing this habit, we will instinctively know the right things to say at the right time when we meet that next great prospect.

When we develop a new habit of meeting one new person every day, this activity will help us build our business naturally. It will be as easy as tying our shoes.

Habits work for us effortlessly in the background. We don't have to struggle with making a new decision every time we need to perform this activity.

Habits are our friends.

Every day, meet one new person.

Some of these people will become friends.

And then, some of our friends will share our passion for our products and our business. People like doing business with their friends.

HABIT #3: PROMOTE EVENTS.

No skills? No confidence? Don't have any prospects?

Don't let these initial obstacles stop us.

Instead, we can promote events while learning the skills of our network marketing business.

Few people enter network marketing with the perfect set of circumstances. Most of us have time limitations, skills from a different profession, or perhaps, a bit of doubt about our chances of success.

Promoting events is our path around our initial challenges.

It doesn't matter if we start with lots of advantages or disadvantages. Anyone can promote events.

So let's see why event promotion can make a network marketing business grow for anyone.

WHY WE SHOULD PROMOTE EVENTS.

#1. It is a lonely world out there.

We join our business, return home, and start our business alone in a world of negative prospects. Discouragement can set in. Doubt can set in. And when we are new, we need support even more.

How do we rejuvenate our attitude? Go to events!

It is easier to believe when we're surrounded by fellow believers.

What if we enrolled across the kitchen table? Or what if we joined our business while having a conversation on our computer screen? In that case, we only saw our sponsor. We didn't see the big picture and support of a team. Events expose us to a bigger vision of what we can be.

Events create belief in the future. When our belief is low, prospects notice our lack of confidence. When our belief is high, prospects feel attracted to our personal enthusiasm and conviction for our business.

#2. Belief is easy after we see or experience a reality.

Belief is difficult before experiencing a reality.

For example, imagine an employee who is hoping for a promotion. While waiting and hoping, it was easy to feel doubt.

However, after receiving the promotion, the employee's belief is confirmed. Yes, it is much easier to believe after the experience.

So how does an event help us believe in our future success?

First, we may see someone at the event with a similar background. If we are an accountant, it would be natural to relate to a speaker at the event who is also an accountant. Now we have more outside proof that we can be successful in our business.

Second, we may see someone of a different background. We think, "That person isn't so special. If that person can do it, I can do it. I am better-qualified. I have more energy. I have more drive to succeed."

Seeing is believing.

#3. In the beginning, we might believe that success is "outside" of us.

We hope that external events will make us successful. Why? Because in the beginning, we feel that we don't have the skills or knowledge to be successful just from our own efforts. We are new.

But what happens at events? A new tool is introduced. A new product is introduced. Or, we learn a new skill - maybe how to talk to people better. These "external" factors sound exciting. We believe that these external factors can help move us forward.

What happens when we believe more? We perform better.

#4. Momentum.

Events attract new prospects and new distributors. These new people create excitement. Excitement leads to action.

And isn't excitement for our business another great habit to create?

Let's ask ourselves, "What is easier: Building with momentum, or without momentum?" The answer is obvious.

#5. Recognition.

Most events have recognition. Anyone can sit in the audience and clap for someone else's achievement. But what about us? What are we thinking?

We are human. Humans crave recognition. We start visualizing ourselves onstage receiving recognition at the next event.

Why?

Think about how much recognition and appreciation we get at work. At home. From our friends. The answer? Not enough. We all crave more.

"A soldier will fight long and hard for a bit of colored ribbon."

—Napoleon Bonaparte.

#6. Social proof.

"Did I make a good decision?" When we are new, doubt lingers in our heads. Attending events validates that we made a good decision. We are surrounded by people who made a similar decision.

Doubt feeds procrastination. The fewer obstacles we face, the faster we can build up momentum.

#7. Peer pressure.

We meet new friends at events. So what happens at the next event? Do we want to be seen at the same rank or achievement with no growth in our business? Of course not. Do we want to be at the same level of achievement for several consecutive events? Definitely not.

Peer pressure gives us an extra boost of external motivation.

#8. One story can change a life.

Many stories are shared onstage at events. We don't know

which speaker or story will resonate with us or our downline. There are many examples in network marketing of people going to an event, hearing a story that touches their hearts, and then making a commitment to build their business. This defining moment changed their lives and their family's lives forever.

#9. We must seek out our dream.

Our dream business will not show up just because we spend a few evenings a week chatting on social media.

Again, seeing is believing. This simple exercise can make a permanent impression in our minds.

First, we attend the event.

Second, we look around at the crowd and imagine everyone is on our team. This creates a feeling of excitement and commitment. We are creating our vision of the future.

Can we get that feeling by watching a video? Reading a book? Sitting at home alone staring at a computer screen? No.

To create this solid belief in our minds, we have to experience the event. This holds true not only for us, but for every team member we have. Events expand our brain so that we have the capacity to be more and earn more.

#10. Third-party influence.

We hear the same message from our local sponsor and leaders. But when a third party sends us that message, it makes an impression. I don't know why we give more credence to strangers, but it is a natural human tendency.

The opportunity, the products, and the effects our business has on other people's lives seem so much more exciting when we hear it from others.

#11. Leverage.

We have a busy schedule. Work, family, and countless obligations fill our week. So how can we have time to sit down with our team and transfer our belief and passion for our business? That can be difficult.

But when we get our team to a major event, we leverage not only time, but also the third-party influence. Allow events to transfer beliefs quickly and efficiently to our team.

As an added bonus, our team members realize they don't have to be the experts. All they have to do is to get their team to the next event.

#12. The power of community.

Imagine these two communities:

1. Dissatisfied co-workers grumbling at the coffee machine. They hate their job. They hate their commute. They talk about the negatives in their lives.

2. Positive network marketers on a path of self-improvement happily chatting after a meeting.

No comparison.

One of the biggest secrets of our business is that people love our community. Associating with us is better than hanging around their negative in-laws, their complaining co-workers, and small-minded friends. Listening to negative 24-hour news channels, reading depressing newspapers ... we just want a break from the drama of everyday life.

We look forward to the community of our new friends in network marketing.

What make communities more powerful and bonded?

Shared experiences.

Attending events together bonds us into a positive, excited community that looks forward to a better future. We will relive memories of trips to the company convention or regional events with our community.

For many, the new social life, friends, and experiences of big events mean more than the income potential of network marketing.

IS CREATING A HABIT TO PROMOTE EVENTS WORTH IT?

Absolutely. Sure, it takes an investment of time and money to attend an event. But how big is the payoff? Huge.

Let me tell you my story from when I was 18 years old.

Dallas, Texas changed my life.

When I first started in 1994. I heard the phrase, "Get to the next event." The next big event was in Dallas, Texas, just over a four-hour drive away.

Not only did they tell me to get to the next event, but they also gave me this life-changing advice:

"If you want to grow your business big, bring a new distributor with you to the event."

I thought, "Perfect. I have to drive there anyway, so I just need to find someone on my team who wants to go."

Easy. Randy was my friend and also a distributor. While he never wanted to work the business full-time as a career, he did love the community of positive friends and associates.

So we packed up the car and went to Dallas. Our first event was incredible. We felt inspired, motivated, and full of enthusiasm. This was definitely better than those boring days in high school.

On our trip back home from Dallas, all we could talk about was the great time we had at the event. We talked about the speakers, the atmosphere, what we learned, and the new friends. We had plenty to talk about and our spirits were high.

And guess what?

The next event was only a month away. We figured we had plenty of time to fill multiple cars with new distributors for the upcoming event.

That was our master plan. Did it work?

No.

One month later, it was only Randy and me in the car going to Dallas for the event.

Luckily, we always had a new event in our upcoming calendar. My business started to grow. Later that year at our annual convention, I walked into the lunch area and ... I had 65 team members attending!

Fast-forward one more year and I had over 800 team members attending the annual convention. Was I excited? That would be an understatement. Having over 800 team members at a convention was bigger than my wildest dreams from my first event.

Now, it took a lot of effort to get 800 team members to attend the annual convention, but it all started by committing to the first event. Most importantly, Randy and I didn't quit when things didn't go as planned.

So what did I do to make this happen?

I was young with little or no influence. Most of my friends and contacts were young too. I was just learning the business bit by bit.

But my real secret?

I promoted events.

Anyone, young or old, new or experienced, can promote events. We are asking people to come to an event. They won't be judging us. Instead, they will be judging the upcoming event. And that is why it is so important for us to build up the value and excitement of the next event to them.

You never know who you will meet.

Many years later, a leader in my organization hosted his own event. Excellent! When leadership duplicates, good things happen.

One issue, though. This event fell on my wedding anniversary.

Normally this wouldn't be a problem, as my wife is very supportive. We like to go to events. But this time, we had an infant at home.

Should I stay home with the family and celebrate our wedding anniversary, or should I go to the event? Well, we can make any excuse to avoid going to an event. This excuse would be good enough to stay home.

However, something inside me told me to go and support my team. I promised my wife we would celebrate our anniversary before and after I went to the event.

Well, the weekend event was great. Now, I consider myself low-key, approachable, and very down-to-earth. But when we speak onstage, some people think we are famous and difficult to approach.

So right before I left to catch my flight home, I met a brand-new distributor on my team. She seemed a little nervous about meeting me. Now, she rode a Greyhound bus for 22 hours to get to the event. That is impressive. She told herself, "I am coming to this event and I will meet as many leaders as I can."

Turned out that she lived near Dallas, Texas. Yes, I love Dallas. Well, I quickly asked for her contact information and told her I would contact her the next time I held a meeting in the Dallas area.

A few months later I called her to say, "I will be doing a meeting in Dallas. Would you please come?"

After a long pause, she reluctantly agreed.

What happened?

She showed up at the meeting with four distributors and eight guests. She brought the most guests for the entire meeting, yet she had the shortest notice of anyone attending. I can't think of a time when I brought eight guests to a meeting. Impressive.

Curious about how she got eight guests to come, I asked how she did it. She replied, "The timing was right. I was about to quit. That is why I paused on the telephone when you invited me to come. But after hanging up the telephone, I got excited. A few weeks earlier my work supervisor notified me that I could either retire early, or risk losing most of my retirement income."

A few months later (things never seem to happen instantly), her business took off. She had leaders in her organization, and she finally found someone who was a bigger go-getter than she was. Now her volume exploded.

Within a year, her one new leadership leg was doing over $2 million in sales every single month. What a great reward for somebody who almost quit.

But the lesson?

I met her at an event.

HOW CAN I MAKE EVENTS WORK FOR ME?

What are some of the skills we can use to get ourselves and others to events?

#1. We always like to be the first to know. Think about human nature. No one wants to be the last to know. When are big announcements made? At events. Events don't always have to be a physical gathering of people. Sure, in-person is better, but sometimes we can turn a simple upcoming conference call into a special event.

#2. Promote the speaker of the upcoming event. The more important or the more knowledgeable the speaker is, the more our distributor or prospect will want to hear the speaker. Talk about the speaker's qualifications, the speaker's accomplishments, or the special skills and information the speaker will present at the event. Better yet, promote the chance to actually meet the speaker in person. We could say, "Here is a chance to meet someone w ho could change your life forever."

#3. Let's be the first person to reserve our ticket for the next big event. This habit sets the example for the rest of the members of our team. Post our ticket for others to see. Our team members will sense our commitment and see how much we value attendance at events. We want to lead by example, not by proclamation.

Duplication? What do we want our team to duplicate? Our lack of commitment? Or, our total commitment to the upcoming event?

#4. Tell success stories about people who attended previous events. We understand concepts better when they're presented in stories. When we hear about others who moved their businesses forward by attending events, we visualize ourselves in that story. We get the feeling that we can do this too.

People love hearing stories. The more great stories we have about previous events, the easier it will be to motivate others to commit to the next event.

#5. Make every event count, no matter how big or small.

Not every event has to be an international conference with thousands or tens of thousands of distributors coming together. An event is simply a group of distributors who want to move forward.

It can be a conference call, a webinar, an opportunity meaning, a Saturday training, a regional rally, or all the way up to the big company conventions.

#6. Remember, there is something at the event for everyone. For some, the event means recognition. For others, the event means a chance to meet new people and enjoy the atmosphere.

THE TWO-SENTENCE MIRACLE.

Many years ago I had to make a 30-second testimonial for a video about the power of events. 30 seconds was definitely not enough time to talk about the mechanics or activities for the event.

So I made a decision. I would appeal to the four basic personality types using two clear sentences. If you aren't familiar with the four personality types, check out the book, *The Four Color Personalities for MLM.*

Here are the two sentences I used:

> "This is the only business where you can make a lot of money, help a lot of people and have a ton of fun doing it. It just makes sense."

That video made my business explode. Why? Because there was something in those two sentences for everyone.

How can you appeal to all four personalities to promote your event?

Just make sure to hit all four personality "hot buttons" every time you promote. Here are the keywords for all your promotions:

1. Party.

2. Money.

3. Information.

4. Help.

Can you see how I addressed these four personalities in those two sentences? Look again.

"This is the only business where you can make a lot of money, help a lot of people and have a ton of fun doing it. It just makes sense."

CREATING THE EVENT PROMOTION HABIT.

Okay. We believe in events. We now know why we should promote events.

Let's make event promotion a habit.

Remember the two sentences from the previous chapter? Well, promoting events doesn't have to be a long, time-consuming effort. Promoting events could be a weekly habit of reminding others of the upcoming event.

What do people remember?

Research shows that people remember more information at the beginning and at the end of our conversation. What does this mean to us?

If we want to leverage our efforts, we should focus on the beginning and the end of our "event" message.

We want to mention our upcoming event during these crucial times.

Think about our emails, our videos, or the beginning and end of our telephone conversations. What can we say to our team members so they realize the power of the upcoming event?

When I first started in network marketing, I realized that my upline leader would sneak in an event promotion at the beginning and end of every conversation. For example, at the end of a telephone conversation he would say:

"See you at the next event."

Or, he would say, "I look forward to meeting you in person at an upcoming event."

I wondered, "Was I being subconsciously programmed to attend the event?" Probably.

Did it make me feel like if I missed the upcoming event, I might be letting my upline leader down? Probably.

But if our intentions are right, and we know it is in our team's best interest to attend the event, our team will always win in the end. This is our job. We want to help our team have the best chance for success.

What are some of the other phrases that we could use?

"I can't wait to see all my leaders on Friday night at the start of the event."

"Friday night is going to be amazing. I am so excited to see everybody that made a decision to attend."

It doesn't cost much to promote an event. It could be a few simple sentences. But we have to remind ourselves to do this often. We can remind ourselves with little yellow notes on our desk. Or maybe a note on the rearview mirror of our car. Maybe we could set a reminder on our phone to promote the event.

Life is measured in experiences, not in years.

We could say, "Life is measured in experiences. We will always remember the incredible experiences in our lives. Let's create a memory together by attending this event. It will be something we will always remember."

What about using recognition?

People love recognition. They don't get recognition from their jobs. Sometimes their families forget about all the sacrifices they make.

So why not recognize people just for making a simple commitment to come to the event?

We can mention people who commit to the event by name. People love to hear their name. Recognition for their commitment to attend the event is important. We could say, "So glad to know that John will be at the event with us. John just joined last week, and we are all eager to meet him at the event."

Many team members will do more for recognition. For example, you could announce a special breakfast before the event. This would be for team members who committed early to the event. Or, maybe a breakfast for team members who have at least one member of their team attending the event.

We could give a certificate of achievement for bringing someone to the event. When visiting team members' homes, I am pleasantly surprised to see that many still have a certificate on their wall that I gave them ten years earlier.

At major events, there is always a lunch break. This is another chance for us to reward people. Maybe we don't want to pay for their lunch, or can't afford to pay for their lunch. However, just an invitation to the luncheon will make people feel special.

If we want to invest a bit of money into our team, here are some awards that we could consider:

- Meals paid.
- Hotel room paid.
- Airfare reimbursement.
- Event ticket reimbursement.
- A ticket for their spouse to attend.
- Money to spend at the event.
- A limo ride to an evening out together.

What would a team member have to do to qualify for one of these awards? Here are some suggestions:

- Sponsor a new team member.
- Create a certain amount of retail sales.
- Have one or more team members attend the event.
- Bring some guests to the next opportunity meeting.
- Have one home product party.
- Be present on four consecutive conference training calls.

What if we wanted to invest more into promotion?

At one event, I went all-out to give incentives to team members who went up in rank. All they had to do was move up one level in the compensation plan. If they achieved this, their airfare, hotel, transportation, and all meals were paid for.

But what made the biggest difference?

I added spending money for the event.

It wasn't a lot of spending money. But it was cash. People love the feeling of cash. It is different than receiving a gift card; cash feels real. At this event, I went to the bank and withdrew one dollar bills. I put 100 one dollar bills in a stack and wrapped them. This made it fun to present stacks of cash to people. Everyone wanted their picture taken while receiving the cash.

To make this even more memorable, I created a custom photo album with pictures of people receiving the cash. The photo album cost less than $50. The team treasured these albums.

We will always have new members who are just beginning their careers. They may be desperate to earn more money, and find it difficult to come to an event. We could offer them an incentive that could pay for their entire event. If they have the desire, they will work hard to achieve this incentive.

What if we don't have a budget to promote the event?

Remember recognition? We can offer recognition to team members who:

1. Are the first to register for the event.

2. Have the most personally-sponsored team members attending the event.

3. Have the most volume for the month coming into the event.

4. Have distributed the most invitations to the event.

We can give this recognition on social media, in newsletters, in a video, announce it at meetings, announce it on conference calls, and more.

If most of our team members are local, we could have a special bowling night out for people who have already purchased their event tickets.

Promote pre-event planning sessions.

At the end of our weekly teleconference training call we could say, "After this call, we have a special call for all team members who have purchased their event tickets. This free event planning call is special."

Some team members will want to get their event ticket now just to be on these pre-event planning calls.

Short videos.

We have short attention spans. The good news is this means our videos can be extremely short. We don't need a long script or an outline. Just a simple 15-second or 30-second video might be all we need to promote our event.

Nowadays it is easy to have a professional-looking video. We don't need a big studio or fancy production facilities.

Just grab our smartphone and we are in business. People relate to us as real people even in our amateur video. Simply worry about getting our video message out there.

A little trick to hold people's attention?

At the beginning of our video announce how long the video will be. For example, "In the next 20 seconds, I want to tell you why I am going to the event."

Most people can hang on for 20 seconds. They know how long our video will be, so they won't be anxious, wondering how long our video will last.

In this video, our excitement and passion will show. Remember, our viewers will pick up on visual clues that tell them if we are sincere or not.

People are addicted to "new."

Think about any 24-hour news channel. What do they focus on? Whatever is new. The newest drama in the world. The latest event. The news channels love to say that something is "breaking news."

Did the old news suddenly go away? No. Did the old news get fixed? No. But people are not interested in old news. They only like new.

The easiest way to promote an event is to say there will be new information. This could be new information about the products, an event, a company trip, an incentive, etc. People will love to hear our news if it's actually new.

So when announcing our upcoming conference call, we can say, "And we will have some exciting news on the call." Promoting what is new just makes it easier.

And don't prejudge. We don't know what will motivate certain team members to come. Some come to the events for emotional reasons. Others for social reasons. Still others for logical reasons.

Maybe our "new" information will not earn us money immediately. However, the information might be just the trigger that helps a team member make the commitment to come to the event.

Remember ... now.

Most people can only see the short term. We can preach long-term vision, long-term goals, and huge dreams, but for most people? They worry about today and maybe tomorrow. In their minds, the event is too far away to worry about. How can we help them see the short-term benefits of the event?

By telling them the feeling they will get when they commit to the event. Let them know the feeling of anticipation they'll experience when they have their own personal ticket.

Or, we can simply let our team know about the immediate benefit of participating in the pre-event planning calls with other team members.

Don't forget what we accomplished.

When we are at an event, we want everyone on our team to return. We want to build on our current base of event attendees. What can we do to make sure this happens?

If there is another event announced, we want to make sure everyone purchases a ticket immediately. Let them know that they can post their picture on social media with their new event ticket. This will drive belief in their team members about the power of events.

People don't want to be "left behind." We are social. We want to feel like we are part of a group. Our excitement about our business is at an all-time high at an event. This is a great time to remind ourselves to repeat the experience.

People want to follow leaders who are going places. We should be that leader.

What if we don't have events?

If our company or team doesn't have events, then events start with us. We have to take that first step.

If we are new, maybe our first event is a special online training. No cost on our part. We just make the personal effort to promote the event. We can't let a lack of events hold us back.

Events may be more important to us than to our team.

Let's keep in mind that many of our team members are part-time. They have busy lives. Our business may not be the entire focus of their day. So what do we have to do?

Remind our team of our upcoming events. That is why the habit of weekly event promotion will move our teams forward.

OUR WEEKLY EVENT HABIT CHECKLIST.

One way won't fit everyone. We need to choose an event promotion habit that works for us.

Here are ten habit ideas we can choose from.

1. Hand out event flyers to people we meet. This is good for getting prospects to attend an opportunity event.

2. Ask one team member a week to come and join us at the next big event.

3. Put a note on our refrigerator to remind us to call someone on Friday night to promote the upcoming event.

4. Tell one event story a week to a team member.

5. Promote and edify the speaker of our next event to someone this week.

6. Instead of posting our picture, post a picture of our next event ticket on social media.

7. Memorize and utilize the "two-sentence miracle phrase."

"This is the only business where you can make a lot of money, help a lot of people and have a ton of fun doing it. It just makes sense."

Practice that phrase once every day before returning home from work.

8. Make the signature file of our emails: "See you at our next event." Use this phrase in every conversation with our team.

9. On social media, or in our newsletter, post and update the names of team members who already have their tickets.

10. Say to people, "Life is more than repeating the same day over and over. Let's make the first weekend next month something different. Let's experience the event together."

ONLY THREE HABITS???

Well, let's be realistic. It will take time to create these first three habits in our lives. Habits don't happen overnight. We will need focus and repetition.

But we should ask ourselves this question: "What would happen to my network marketing career if I made these three habits permanent?"

I think we could all agree the results would be outstanding. And what would happen if our downline adopted these permanent habits? We would be proud of our downline if they:

- Did personal development every day.
- Met one new person every day.
- Promoted events weekly.

Now we have the beginning of a solid organization that can start to duplicate.

Can I work on additional habits now?

Certainly. These are not the only three habits network marketers would like to learn.

However, we generally have better success by focusing on one habit at a time.

It is better to spend three weeks creating one new permanent habit, then to try to create 20 new habits simultaneously.

Because there are such a variety of goals for network marketers, there will be many different habits we may want to develop. For the rest of this book, we will expand on additional methods and ideas for creating habits.

One method of creating habits will not fit every person. We can choose what feels right for us.

Another thought about the various ways of creating habits:

If the method you choose to create your habit fills you with dread and stress, consider looking for a different way to create that desired habit. It is hard to focus on repetition when you hate the activity with a passion.

"I really want to take habit creation seriously."

There are huge books and piles of research about habits. This book isn't part of the science of habit creation. This book is only about three starting habits for network marketers.

If you wish to dig deeper into habits, we love S.J. Scott's books. His books expand on a variety of different habits, including … exercise. His books are easy to read, and just focus on one area at a time. You can also go to his blog at http://www.DevelopGoodHabits.com.

Here are some additional great books on habits:

1. *Mini Habits: Smaller Habits, Bigger Results* by Stephen Guise.

2. *The Power of Habit: Why We Do What We Do in Life and Business* by Charles Duhigg.

3. *The 7 Habits of Highly Effective People* by Stephen Covey

CAN HABITS MAKE MY DREAMS COME TRUE?

Ah, that is the secret.

Yes. Regular habits move us toward our goals.

Here is a little five-step strategy that makes achieving our goals easier.

#1. Choose a goal.

It is hard to point ourselves in the right direction if we don't know where we are going. Having a goal tells our subconscious mind, "Hey, look out for opportunities or resources that might help us get closer to our goal."

For instance, if you had a bad meal racing through your intestines, you have set a goal. You want to find the restrooms quickly. This tells your subconscious mind to notice every public restroom sign. Your subconscious mind is aware that this is an urgent goal.

#2. Figure out which habit will make our goal happen ... automatically.

Let's do an exercise example.

Try to make a conscious decision to go to the gym and work out every day. Chances are, this will fail. We come home from a long day at work. The stress drained our willpower supply. Now we want to make a decision to go work out at the gym. Well, our old habits will take over. We grab the remote control, a bowl of ice cream, and prepare for five hours of mind-numbing television.

That isn't going to work. We need something more automatic.

So instead, we decide that climbing stairs, lots of stairs, will make exercise happen automatically. How do we do this?

Imagine we live in a two-story house with a basement. We put our television, computer and home office on the top floor, and our food and snacks in the basement.

Every time we are hungry, we have to trudge down two flights of stairs for a snack, and two flights of stairs back up. That is a start.

Want to improve this?

We make a rule that we must drink two glasses of water for every 30 minutes of television or computer time. We disable the upstairs toilets and the main floor toilets, so the only working toilet is in the basement. Lots of automatic trips up and down the stairs are in our future.

By rearranging our circumstances, we don't have to use willpower. Our circumstances can substitute for willpower. That gives us the edge.

#3. Throw in a little reward motivation.

If we have an addiction to chocolate chip cookies, say to ourselves, "I can take a bite of a chocolate chip cookie every time I do five pushups."

We are going to build some strong arms!

Want to have more fun?

Then plan to celebrate your success with others. Group pressure will help us perform when we feel weak. We don't want to let others down.

#4. Throw in a little penalty motivation.

If we don't go downstairs at least once every 30 minutes, we can't continue watching television or surfing the Internet. A kitchen alarm or computer alarm makes this easy to implement.

#5. Know the reason for our goal.

If we have strong emotional reasons, this gets easier. For example, imagine that we want to lose weight for our class reunion. We don't want to wear a tent to the event. Thinking about wearing a tent could make it a bit easier to go up and down those stairs every day. Hey, maybe we could chant during our stair time, "No more tent!"

Logical reasons are nice, but emotional reasons are more powerful.

Every little bit helps.

Our goal is to get the odds on our side. We want to have every advantage we can when creating a habit.

Remember, habits will happen almost effortlessly, even if we are a bit tired.

And this is how we can develop the habit of success that we want.

SO WHAT ABOUT MY NETWORKING BUSINESS?

Imagine we are just starting, and the odds are against us.

First, we have a long commute going to our job and back home.

Second, our spouse wants us to spend more time with the family.

Third, we don't have time to consistently build our business because we are also busy remodeling the house.

The reasons "why we can't do it" seem overwhelming.

But remember this ...

Some people will join our team, just because we showed up.

Earlier in this book, we pointed out that in a group of 100 people, five people might never join. Society crushed their spirits, their bosses sucked out their will to live, and they don't believe anything good can happen to them. Not much we can do here.

But out of those same 100 people, five people might join just because we showed up! It is the right time in their lives for a business opportunity, and we were there.

So let's put the five-step strategy to work to kick-start our network marketing business.

#1. Choose a goal.

This is easy. We want to personally sponsor five people on our team.

#2. Figure out which habit will make this goal happen automatically.

Looks like we will have to contact a lot of people, so that we can have conversations with 100 people. How are we going to do that?

Because of our time limitations, this is what we decide to do. On our way home from work, we are going to stop our car and call three people. This could take one minute if we reach no one. Or, it could take 10 minutes if we connect with one person out of those three calls. So, not long.

In our case, we might just check with them by saying, "Hey, I'm tired of commuting every day. I want to start my own part-time business and eventually work from home. Just wanted to know if you felt the same way."

Now, that was easy for us to say. We could write those three short sentences on a piece of paper, and tape it to the dashboard of our car. This would be an easy habit to create. Just make three phone calls on the way home, and we know exactly what to say! No rejection here. Easy to do.

We don't care if we connect with three people, or no people. This is just a little habit we can do every day. Over time, we will eventually talk to 100 people.

#3. Throw in a little reward motivation.

Tell ourselves, "Hey, if I actually connect with a 'live' person, I can get an iced latte to enjoy for the rest of my drive." This way we will at least try to connect with people because we love iced lattes. And maybe we would even cheat a little. If we didn't connect on our three calls, we might try a fourth call. We really love those iced lattes.

#4. Throw in a little penalty motivation.

Tell ourselves, "If I don't make these three calls, no television or Internet time tonight." This could be brutal! How can we go on in life if we don't see Facebook pictures of what our friends ate for lunch?

#5. Know the reason for our goal.

That's easy. We waste one hour commuting in the morning. We waste one hour commuting in the evening. This is all lost time from our lives. Commuting makes us feel sick to our stomachs.

Before we start our three calls, we say to ourselves, "I hate commuting! Bring on the prospects!"

5 STEPS.

In the previous five-step strategy, which step will be the most important?

Step #2: Figure out which habit will make our goal happen automatically.

Making this habit easy is the key.

Remember, let's start our habits small. The less willpower needed to start our habit, the greater our chances of success.

We can always increase the scope and intensity of our new habit. But, do this slowly. Staying close to or within our comfort zone means we will be more consistent.

A change of strategy.

Instead of focusing on a final goal, we will concentrate on creating a habit that will get us there ... naturally.

Goals are big and complicated in our minds. We may think globally, but we only act locally. The accumulation of simple habits makes goals easier to achieve.

For example, think of a giant pizza. Instead of trying to consume the pizza in one large bite, we will start with one slice at a time. Then, we will take one bite of that first slice of pizza. Then, another bite. Eventually, we will finish that first slice of pizza and will start on the second slice of pizza.

This is easy. Why?

We've already mastered the automatic habit of biting and chewing. All we need to do is to get that first slice of pizza close to our mouth.

Over time, we will eat the entire pizza.

The simple act of walking.

How about another example?

Our goal (Step #1) is to walk at least ten minutes a day. Yes, that is starting pretty small, but we have to start somewhere.

Ask ourselves, "What habit will make my goal happen automatically?"

That's easy.

We park our car five minutes away from work. That means we will walk five minutes from the car to work, and five minutes from work to the car. Total walking time? Ten minutes.

Personal development.

Imagine we want to build an "attitude of gratitude" in our subconscious minds. What can we do to make this almost automatic?

Let's say having coffee and a donut for our morning break is our favorite part of the day. All we have to do is to give ourselves this challenge:

"No morning coffee break until we have appreciated or thanked someone today."

We never want to miss our coffee and donut, so we will appreciate or thank someone every day before our coffee break. Do this once a day and soon we'll have a lifelong habit. Personal development is easy with habits.

Our new habit is to give one person, any person, a simple compliment today. Giving compliments is a great way to develop a friendlier personality. We won't have to worry about rejection or hurting feelings. People are so compliment-starved that the most common reaction to our compliment is shock! Compliment recipients may just freeze in place with their mouths open.

But we don't have to limit our complimenting to just the morning. We could make a habit of complimenting others throughout the day.

We might try a few easy compliments such as:

"Nice car. I like the color."

"What's that scent you're wearing? It's quite nice."

"Great suggestion. I will put it to use right away."

"Thanks for the _____. It was very thoughtful of you."

"I like the way you arranged your desk."

"Cute dog. Does it do tricks?"

After a few weeks, we can increase our compliments to two a day.

See how easy this is? Small bites, little habits, 100% success.

Meeting one new person a day.

To make this goal automatic, what can we do?

How about smiling and saying "Hi" to everyone we meet? Eventually, someone will say "Hi" back to us, and start a brief conversation. We will smile and say "Hi" every day until we get that first conversation.

Promoting events.

To make this goal automatic, what can we do?

Print some postcard-sized announcements of the upcoming event. Place these cards near our keys. Every time we pick up our keys in the morning, we take an announcement card. Better yet, we could take more than one announcement card.

Then, during the day, make sure we give someone an announcement card while telling them about our upcoming event.

MORNING PEOPLE / NIGHT PEOPLE.

What happens if our new habit is too far outside our comfort zone or natural ability?

We will give up too soon.

Of course we want massive changes instantly. But trying to change too much too soon could mean impending failure.

We need less motivation and willpower when our new habits don't require massive changes in our lives. Small steps. One step at a time.

Here is an example.

Biological prime time.

We have a certain time of the day that is best for us. We call this our "biological prime time." Things are easier during this time of day. Motivation happens naturally.

We should ask ourselves, "What is my biological prime time?"

Morning people.

Some people are naturally "morning people." They wake up happy. They feel good. They have energy to burn. Their brain releases feel-good chemicals from the moment they open their eyes until early evening. Then they crash.

Are we morning people?

If we are, why not attempt new habits in the morning when we are at our best? We could exercise, write down goals, read books, and organize our workplace ... while feeling fantastic.

Why not join those early morning breakfast networking events? We could do that five days a week, or maybe six days a week!

So what do we do in the evening when we don't have any more willpower and energy? We can do minor administrative tasks or brush our teeth before we collapse into bed.

Evening people.

Are we evening people?

Want to feel depressed? All we have to do is to set an exercise goal every morning. We will use up an entire day's worth of willpower just to make that happen. Mornings are our time for mindless tasks. It might take several cups of coffee before we feel conscious.

And evenings? Phone calls, meetings, planning the next day ... this is our best time to think and execute. If we want to develop one new habit, why not choose a new habit that will fit into our evening schedule when we are feeling great?

If we are night owls, we can make calls to prospects in different time zones. Or, start a late-night training conference call for all the other "night people" in our group.

MAKE A HABIT OF CREATING VALUE FOR OTHERS.

Why do people refuse to return our telephone calls? Later, when we see them, they create a list of excuses why they didn't get back to us.

But what is the real reason they refused to call us back?

Because they didn't feel like we were adding value to their lives. They perceived us as "takers," only interested in what we can take for ourselves. For example:

- We want them to join our business so that we can earn more money.
- We want them to buy our products so we earn more commissions.
- We want them to send us the names of their friends so that their friends can benefit our personal success.
- We want them to come to our meeting so that we have more attendees.
- We want them to host a meeting with their friends so we can sell more of our products and services.

Our friends and contacts are just being human. We act that way too. We don't want to call back people that we perceive as "takers."

Is there another way?

Of course. Instead of being a "taker," we could become a "giver." People love "givers" because "givers" **add** value to the lives of others.

Now we are more concerned about our prospects' welfare than we are about our personal welfare. This means we will constantly look for resources to enhance our prospects' lives.

Here are some easy examples of resources we can pass on to others.

#1. Maybe our prospect's picture is in the local newspaper today. Why not cut out the picture and send it him? Many people love to have a collection of photos that remind them of their accomplishments.

#2. Forward our prospect a special article that relates to the prospect's passion or hobby.

#3. Notify our prospect of a special sale.

#4. Notify the prospect of a special conference coming to her city.

#5. Pass on the latest tax-saving tip.

#6. Recommend the best doctor, dentist or lawn care specialist.

#7. Let others know that your prospect is selling his house. Spread the word.

#8. Ask your prospect if her daughter is selling fund-raising cookies again this year.

#9. Put your prospect in contact with a new friend who has a similar interest or passion.

#10. Offer to help load the truck when your prospect moves.

Got the idea? Providing value is just being a friend. That is what friends do. Everyone welcomes a "giver" when he or she enters the room. Everyone gives a sigh of relief when a "taker" leaves the room. That is a hint. Adding value to people's lives is not only good for business, but it's also part of becoming a good person.

Can we make this a habit?

Why not? What if we went out of our way every day to deliver more value to one person, two people, or even three people? Some interesting changes happen.

First, our personal attitude about our business changes. We start feeling that our business adds value to other people's lives.

Second, we have more friends. People love to join and help their true friends in business.

Third, we look at our environment differently. Instead of looking at places and things only from our personal selfish viewpoint, we look for value in everything we see. Our perspective of the world changes. We see opportunities and resources everywhere. This mindset change helps our personal belief that the world provides unlimited resources for our use. We only need to open our eyes and observe.

What would be good trigger questions to help us remember to add value?

"Before I send this email, does this email also contain something that benefits the reader?"

"Before I make this telephone call, do I have at least one tip or resource that I can give to the person I am calling?"

"Before I approach these cold prospects, do I have something of value I can give to the prospects regardless of their interest in my business?"

Make a habit of asking these questions before interacting with prospects. We will build character. We will feel better. Our prospects will feel better.

Over time, our business will reflect the results of this habit.

UPGRADE OUR ASSOCIATIONS AND ENVIRONMENT.

Associations are a crutch. A good crutch. Our surroundings influence us. If we hang around our old high school friends who smoke and drink, there is a good chance we will pick up those habits.

Stand by the coffee machine with negative coworkers. If they complain about everything, we could pick up a negative view of the world.

But what if we associate ourselves with people who eat healthy foods? Or, what if we associate ourselves with people who exercise daily? Of course it will be easier to create that new habit.

Want a little help or boost to create a new habit? Then we should associate ourselves with people who already practice that habit.

Jake Pena has a great saying, "If you hang around four broke people, I guarantee you will be number five."

The Fresh Prince of Bel-Air.

In the early 1990s, there was a show called, *The Fresh Prince of Bel-Air*. The main character, Will, lived in a troubled neighborhood. He was sent to live with his relatives thousands of miles away across the U.S. Living in Bel-Air was a better environment. Eventually Will changed his habits and actions and became more positive.

Do we have to move to a better neighborhood to improve our habits and lives? Of course not. But moving to a more positive environment did make it easier for Will.

In every neighborhood there are people looking to improve themselves. Why not locate these people and associate with them? It is not where we are, but where we are headed that counts. Look for people who are traveling in the direction we want to go.

That's why events are great. We surround ourselves with people who are going in the direction we wish to go. But we are not at an event 24 hours a day, seven days a week. What are we going to do when we go home?

We will upgrade our associations. We want to make it easier to change our habits.

THE HABIT OF BITING OUR TONGUES.

The habit of listening is hard to master. Two main problems:

1. We want to talk. We always look for a break where we can take over the conversation. After all, what we want to say is really, really important. That means we are not listening to the words of the speaker. That creates misunderstanding.

2. We don't process the message behind the words. Our minds are busy organizing and remembering what we want to say next. There is no room in our mind for listening or deciphering the real message from the speaker.

While there are endless books and courses on listening, we can start a better listening habit now. The more practice, the better we get.

What is the reward?

Who do people like better? People who talk a lot, or people who listen? Yes, everyone loves a good listener.

Now, if we are shy, we already have a head start! We might be thinking, "I wonder what I should say next. I don't want to look stupid. Will this person judge me for what I would like to say?"

But, while we are thinking these thoughts, the speaker is impressed. Why? Because the speaker thinks we are listening!

The first secret in listening is to not talk. Here is an easy solution that will make us look much more intelligent than we might actually be.

First, clench your fist.

Second, place your clenched fist below your chin, and push up.

This keeps our mouths shut. We have the appearance of a deep thinker, pondering the supreme intelligence of the speaker.

USE "IF" AND "THEN" TO CREATE HABITS.

Heidi Grant Halvorson writes about using "if" and "then" to trigger action on our new habit. Simply tell ourselves, "If this happens, then I will do this next."

Remember our first habit? We wake up and immediately start playing some personal development audios. That triggers the habit of brushing our teeth, which triggers us to do some squats while brushing. After a while these habits become a natural part of our routine.

Computer programs use the "if-then" routine. If this happens, then automatically do this. Here are some examples that we can use:

- If I eat too much for dessert, then I will take a 15-minute walk.

- If I need to get ready for work, then I will start playing my personal development audio.

- If it is 7:00pm, then I will make prospecting calls for 20 minutes.

- If it is Monday, then I will make a new post on social media.

- If it is time to go to bed, then I will make a list of three things I need to do tomorrow.

The "if-then" triggers an action for our new habit. This is useful so we do not forget our current habits. We all need reminders. Just think of this "if-then" technique as an automatic alarm clock.

MORE IDEAS AND TIPS TO HELP US BUILD OUR NEW HABITS.

Again, choose which tips might feel right for you. We want the result - creating the new habit. The methods or tips we use to get there can be different for everyone.

Jerry Seinfeld's advice.

When Jerry was building his career, he made a goal of writing jokes every day. Every day he wrote, he put a giant "X" on the calendar day.

Could we use this in our business?

Get a giant "year-at-a-glance" calendar and post it on the wall. Imagine we set a goal of talking to one new person a day. Each evening we can put an "X" over that day on our calendar.

We won't want to break the chain. The more days we do this in a row, the worse we will feel if we break the chain.

Nothing like a little external motivation to keep us going.

But what if I fail? What if I miss a day?

Don't panic. It is not the end of the world. We are developing a habit. To prevent ourselves from feeling bad, let's revise our definition of habit. Let's described a habit as, "Something we do most of the time."

So if we didn't make our telephone calls one day, or we fell off our diet one day, let's not punish ourselves. Everyone has missed brushing their teeth at least once.

Instead, just mark the incident as the day we didn't do our normal habit. This will make it easier to continue building our new habit without feeling guilty.

Pressure from your spouse.

We can get our spouse involved and excited about our business by celebrating small achievements. For example, every week that we make 20 follow-up telephone calls, we celebrate by eating out for dinner on Friday night.

If our spouse is looking forward to dinner out on Friday night, and we have not made our 20 follow-up telephone calls, guess who might be giving us a pep talk?

This little habit of celebrating small achievements can keep us on track to build our business.

Follow-up.

Choose a number. Let's say that we are very part-time and only have a few minutes to an hour a day to build our business. In this case, our number could be "1" - the number of prospects that we will follow up with every day.

Not everyone will join on the first exposure to our business. Some take time to think. Others have more pressing obligations. Some have to grow into the mindset of having their own businesses.

We accumulate lots of these prospects the longer we are in our business. Follow-up is necessary. We have to reach out to them to remind them about our opportunity. Their lives are so busy, sometimes they forget to think about where they are going.

Is follow-up hard? No. It could be simple. Some examples:

1. A simple text saying, "Hi. Hope things are well."

2. Sending the prospect a link to an article that is interesting.

3. Asking a prospect if they've tried the sample yet.

4. Letting the prospect know about an important speaker or event.

Oh, wait. Now it's your turn!

The purpose of this book is to create three simple habits and put them into use in our business.

But you might want to know more about the power of habits. So, make sure to check out the books we mentioned earlier. The science of habits is fascinating, and the power of habits can transform our lives.

But for now, let's concentrate on creating the three big habits for network marketers:

1. Personal development.

2. Meet one new person a day.

3. Promote events.

Later, when our three basic habits are automatic, we can expand to more habits to improve our lives.

Have fun developing new habits!

THANK YOU.

Thank you for purchasing and reading this book.

Before you go, would it be okay if we asked a small favor? Would you take just one minute and leave a short review of this book online? Your review can help others choose what they will read next. It would be greatly appreciated by many fellow readers.

I travel the world 240+ days each year.
Let me know if you want me to stop in your
area and conduct a live Big Al training.
BigAlSeminars.com

More Big Al books available at:
BigAlBooks.com

Get the FREE weekly Big Al Report
plus extra bonuses! Sign up today at:
BigAlReport.com

MORE BIG AL BOOKS

The Four Color Personalities for MLM
The Secret Language for Network Marketers

Learn the skill to quickly recognize the four personalities and how to use magic words to translate your message.

Ice Breakers!
How To Get Any Prospect To Beg You For A Presentation

Create unlimited Ice Breakers on-demand. Your distributors will no longer be afraid of prospecting, instead, they will love prospecting.

How To Get Instant Trust, Belief, Influence and Rapport!
13 Ways To Create Open Minds By Talking To The Subconscious Mind

Learn how the pros get instant rapport and cooperation with even the coldest prospects. The #1 skill every new distributor needs.

First Sentences for Network Marketing
How To Quickly Get Prospects On Your Side

Attract more prospects and give more presentations with great first sentences that work.

Big Al's MLM Sponsoring Magic
How to Build a Network Marketing Team Quickly

This book shows the beginner exactly what to do, exactly what to say, and does it through the eyes of a brand-new distributor.

How To Prospect, Sell And Build Your Network Marketing Business With Stories

If you want to communicate effectively, add your stories to deliver your message.

26 Instant Marketing Ideas To Build Your Network Marketing Business

176 pages of amazing marketing lessons and case studies to get more prospects for your business immediately.

How To Build Network Marketing Leaders

Volume One: Step-By-Step Creation Of MLM Professionals

This book will give you the step-by-step activities to actually create leaders.

How To Build Network Marketing Leaders

Volume Two: Activities And Lessons For MLM Leaders

You will find many ways to change people's viewpoints, to change their beliefs, and to reprogram their actions.

Start SuperNetworking!

5 Simple Steps To Creating Your Own Personal Networking Group

Start your own personal networking group and have new, pre-sold customer and prospects come to you.

How to Follow Up With Your Network Marketing Prospects

Turn Not Now Into Right Now!

Use the techniques in this book to move your prospects forward from "Not Now" to "Right Now!"

Complete list at BigAlBooks.com

ABOUT THE AUTHORS

Keith Schreiter has 20+ years of experience in network marketing and MLM. He is the co-author of the books,

- *51 Ways and Places to Sponsor New Distributors: Discover Hot Prospect For Your Network Marketing Business*

- *How to Follow Up With Your Network Marketing Prospects: Turn Not Now Into Right Now*

- *Start SuperNetworking! 5 Simple Steps To Creating Your Own Personal Networking Group*

Keith shows network marketers how to use simple systems to build a stable and growing business.

So, do you need more prospects? Do you need your prospects to commit instead of stalling? Want to know how to engage and keep your group active? If these are the types of skills you would like to master, you will enjoy his "how-to" style.

Keith speaks and trains in the United States, Canada, and Europe.

Tom "Big Al" Schreiter has 40+ years of experience in network marketing and MLM. As the author of the original "Big Al" training books in the late '70s, he has continued to speak in over 80 countries on using the exact words and phrases to get prospects to open up their minds and say "YES."

His passion is marketing ideas, marketing campaigns, and how to speak to the subconscious mind in simplified, practical ways. He is always looking for case studies of incredible marketing campaigns that give usable lessons.

As the author of numerous audio trainings, Tom is a favorite speaker at company conventions and regional events.